HARMONY IN HUES

Unifying Spirituality Across World Religions

Table of Contents

Book Introduction

In a world where divisions and conflicts seem to be the norm, the search for harmony and unity becomes increasingly vital. "Harmony in Hues: Unifying Spirituality Across World Religions" embarks on a transformative journey through the rich tapestry of human spiritual traditions, revealing the interconnectedness that unites all people beyond the boundaries of creed, culture, and geography.

In our pursuit of understanding and peace, it is imperative to recognize the common threads that have woven through the spiritual fabric of humanity since time immemorial. While diverse world religions may appear distinct on the surface, they often share profound underlying principles and values. This book seeks to explore those shared elements that reverberate across religious boundaries, drawing from the profound wisdom of diverse traditions.

The first section of the book delves into the roots of spiritual diversity. From ancient civilizations to the modern-day, humans have sought answers to life's deepest questions. It is here that the quest for meaning and connection with the divine begins, paving the way for the myriad of spiritual paths that grace our world.

Next, the journey takes us into the realm of mysticism and esoteric traditions. These ancient schools of thought, present in various religious practices, delve into the mysteries of existence and transcendence. We explore the transformative experiences and insights that mystics have had throughout history, bridging the gap between the mundane and the sacred.

The book then turns its attention to the major world religions, from monotheistic faiths like Christianity, Islam, and Judaism to the rich philosophies of the East, such as Hinduism and Buddhism. By examining the core beliefs and teachings of these religions, we can identify the common goal of finding peace and harmony within oneself and with others.

Moreover, "Harmony in Hues" honors the wisdom and practices of indigenous cultures that revere the earth as sacred. By reconnecting with nature, these traditions offer valuable insights into sustainable living and the interconnectedness of all life forms.

Throughout the chapters, we encounter the seekers and sages who have dedicated their lives to the pursuit of spiritual enlightenment. From ascetics renouncing worldly possessions to gurus guiding their disciples, their stories inspire and illuminate the path of self-discovery.

Rituals and ceremonies play an essential role in spiritual practices worldwide. As we explore the diverse ways people commune with the divine, we find that these rituals often serve as bridges between the physical and spiritual realms.

As we progress, we discover the power of spiritual symbols that speak a language beyond words. From sacred geometry to iconic representations of deities, symbols hold the potential to unite believers and serve as gateways to the transcendent.

The book also dedicates a chapter to the often-underrepresented role of women in world religions. It illuminates the remarkable contributions of women to their respective spiritual traditions and their efforts to bring about positive change in their communities.

In the contemporary age, scientific discoveries have led to a perceived conflict between science and spirituality. However, this book seeks to harmonize these seemingly disparate realms, revealing that both can enrich our understanding of existence.

With the increasing interconnectedness of our globalized world, interfaith dialogue has become a crucial avenue for building understanding and empathy. This book examines the efforts and achievements of interfaith movements, promoting mutual respect and peaceful coexistence.

"Harmony in Hues" recognizes the need for harmony not only within ourselves but also with the world we inhabit. The spiritual ecology chapter explores the interconnectedness between the well-being of the earth and the well-being of the human soul, urging us to be responsible stewards of our planet.

As we approach the culmination of this spiritual odyssey, we embrace the mystery that dwells within all spiritual paths. Surrendering to the ineffable, we find solace in the presence of something greater than ourselves and kindle the flame of faith in our hearts.

Finally, the book concludes with a vision for a world united in its spiritual diversity. By celebrating the uniqueness of each tradition while recognizing our shared humanity, we lay the groundwork for a future where harmony prevails over discord, and love overcomes division.

Join me in this extraordinary expedition through the vibrant tapestry of human spirituality, where we weave together the many hues of belief and practice into a symphony of harmonious coexistence. Let us embark on a journey that celebrates our shared humanity and lights the path to a world where harmony reigns supreme.

Chapter 1: Exploring the Roots of Spiritual Diversity

In the beginning, before civilizations emerged, humans looked up to the heavens and down to the earth, searching for answers to the mysteries of existence. The sun, the moon, the stars, and the cycles of nature became their first objects of worship. From these primal instincts sprang animism, the belief that all things, animate or inanimate, possess a spirit.

As societies evolved and settled into agricultural communities, the concept of deity and polytheism emerged. Ancient cultures across the globe worshipped a pantheon of gods and goddesses, each representing various aspects of life and nature. From the Egyptian gods to the Greek and Roman deities, these polytheistic systems reflected the multifaceted nature of human experience.

With the rise of great empires and the advancement of written languages, the world witnessed the birth of some of the most influential religions. The Abrahamic faiths, including Judaism, Christianity, and Islam, trace their origins back to the figure of Abraham and share a monotheistic belief in one Almighty God. These religions offered moral guidelines, laws, and scriptures to guide their followers on the path of righteousness.

In the East, the spiritual landscape took on a different hue with the rise of Hinduism, Buddhism, Jainism, and other Dharmic traditions. These philosophical systems emphasize the concepts of karma, dharma, and reincarnation, encouraging individuals to seek liberation from the cycle of birth and death.

As diverse as these traditions may seem, they often share core principles, such as compassion, love, and the pursuit of inner peace. The golden rule, expressed in various forms across religions, advocates treating others as one would wish to be treated.

Throughout history, great spiritual teachers and prophets have emerged, delivering messages of love, wisdom, and hope to their followers. From Moses leading the Israelites to the Promised Land to Jesus Christ's teachings of forgiveness and salvation, and from the Prophet Muhammad's revelations in the Quran to the enlightenment of Siddhartha Gautama, these figures left profound impacts on the course of human spirituality.

Spirituality also found expression in the hearts of those attuned to the rhythms of the natural world. Indigenous cultures held profound reverence for the earth and its creatures, viewing all life as interconnected and sacred. Their ceremonies, rituals, and practices embodied a harmonious relationship with nature, teaching valuable lessons about stewardship and sustainability.

As trade routes expanded and empires flourished, ideas and beliefs flowed across borders, leading to syncretism. Different cultures came into contact, influencing and borrowing from one another, creating unique blends of spiritual practices. This cross-fertilization enriched the spiritual landscape and exemplified the interconnectedness of humanity.

With the advent of science, some questioned the role of spirituality in an increasingly rational world. However, the dialogue between science and spirituality has proven to be enriching rather than adversarial. Many scientists find inspiration in the mysteries of the cosmos, recognizing that the pursuit of knowledge and the pursuit of spiritual wisdom are not mutually exclusive.

As we explore the roots of spiritual diversity, we discover that the human quest for meaning and connection transcends the boundaries of time and space. While the world's religions may differ in their rituals and symbols, at their core, they share a common yearning for understanding and transcendence. It is this shared aspiration that forms the foundation of "Harmony in Hues," a testament to the beauty of spiritual diversity and the unifying power of the human spirit.

Chapter 2: The Common Threads of Human Spirituality

In the vast tapestry of human spirituality, there are threads that traverse across cultures, epochs, and belief systems. These commonalities unite humanity in its search for higher meaning and purpose. As we delve deeper into the shared essence of spiritual experience, we find that certain themes reoccur, transcending the boundaries that might otherwise divide us.

One of the most pervasive threads in the fabric of spirituality is the concept of the Divine or the Ultimate Reality. While the names and attributes ascribed to the Divine vary across religions, the underlying notion of a higher power that governs the universe remains a constant. Whether it is the Christian God, the Islamic Allah, the Hindu Brahman, or the Buddhist Nirvana, seekers of truth have always felt drawn to something greater than themselves.

Connected to the idea of the Divine is the longing for a deeper connection with this transcendent reality. Throughout history, individuals have sought communion with the Divine through prayer, meditation, chanting, or rituals. These practices serve as conduits for believers to experience a sense of awe, wonder, and oneness with the sacred.

The pursuit of inner transformation and personal growth is another shared aspect of spirituality. Across different traditions, spiritual seekers strive to cultivate virtues such as compassion, love, humility, and forgiveness. The journey of self-discovery often involves overcoming ego-driven desires and cultivating a deeper understanding of one's true nature.

A central theme in spiritual teachings is the principle of moral conduct and ethical living. The concept of right and wrong, expressed through various moral codes, serves as a compass to navigate the complexities of life. While the specifics may differ, the underlying message remains consistent: leading a virtuous life is essential for spiritual growth and harmonious coexistence.

Another common thread in human spirituality is the recognition of suffering and the quest for liberation from it. Whether it is the Buddhist concept of dukkha or the Christian understanding of sin, all major religions acknowledge the existence of suffering and propose paths towards liberation and salvation. The desire to alleviate suffering and attain a state of peace and bliss unites humanity in its shared struggle.

Throughout history, sages and mystics have recounted experiences of transcendence and divine revelation. These profound encounters with the numinous often result in spiritual insights and revelations that serve as guidance for their followers. The language used to describe these experiences may vary, but the underlying transformative power remains universal.

An essential aspect of spiritual practice is the sense of community and belonging it fosters. Religious gatherings, temples, churches, mosques, and other places of worship serve not only as spaces for ritual but also as hubs for social interaction and support. These communities offer a sense of belonging, solidarity, and shared purpose, enriching the spiritual journey.

As humans grapple with the transient nature of life, the concept of life after death emerges as a recurring motif in spiritual beliefs. Whether it is the cycle of reincarnation in Hinduism and Buddhism or the promise of heaven and hell in Abrahamic faiths, the belief in an afterlife provides comfort and hope in the face of mortality.

Throughout the ages, sacred scriptures have served as guiding lights for spiritual seekers. From the Bible to the Quran, the Bhagavad Gita to the Tao Te Ching, these texts hold the wisdom of ages and offer timeless insights into the human condition. The reverence for scripture as a source of divine guidance unites believers across diverse faiths.

Ultimately, the common threads of human spirituality highlight the interconnectedness of all religious traditions. They speak to the shared aspirations, fears, and hopes that bind us together as one human family. By recognizing these unifying elements, we open the door to dialogue, understanding, and mutual respect, paving the way for a world where harmony and cooperation prevail over discord and division.

In the subsequent chapters of "Harmony in Hues," we will delve deeper into the richness of specific spiritual traditions and explore how they contribute to the tapestry of global spirituality. By embracing the diversity and commonality of our spiritual expressions, we embark on a transformative journey towards a world of unity and understanding.

Chapter 3: Ancient Wisdom: Mysticism and Esoteric Traditions

In the realms of spirituality, the path of mysticism and esoteric wisdom holds a special place. Mysticism, derived from the Greek word "mystikos," meaning "initiated," refers to a direct and intimate experience of the divine. Throughout history, mystics have sought to transcend the limitations of the material world and attain union with the transcendent reality.

Mystical traditions exist in various cultures and religions, each with its unique practices and insights. From the Sufi mystics of Islam to the Kabbalists of Judaism and the Christian contemplatives, these seekers of truth have endeavored to pierce the veils of the ordinary and glimpse the mysteries of existence.

One of the central themes in mystical teachings is the idea of the spiritual journey or the ascent of the soul. Mystics often speak of the soul's longing to return to its source, to reunite with the Divine from which it originated. This yearning for union drives the mystic to seek deeper truths, turning inward through meditation, prayer, and self-reflection.

The ancient mystics recognized that the material world is but a reflection of deeper spiritual realities. They explored the symbolism hidden within sacred texts, art, and nature, believing that these symbols contain profound spiritual truths. This esoteric knowledge was often reserved for the initiated few, and the mysteries were passed down through secret teachings and rituals.

Esoteric traditions, such as Hermeticism and alchemy, emerged as paths of spiritual transformation through the understanding of hidden correspondences in the universe. The alchemists sought to transmute base metals into gold as a metaphor for the transformation of the soul from its impure state to its divine essence. These traditions blended spiritual insights with practical knowledge of the natural world, emphasizing the interconnectedness of all things.

In mystical experiences, the boundaries of the self dissolve, and the mystic may enter states of altered consciousness. They may experience a sense of oneness with the cosmos or undergo profound realizations about the nature of reality. These encounters with the divine are often ineffable, defying ordinary language and understanding.

The works of famous mystics, such as Rumi, Meister Eckhart, Ibn Arabi, and Hildegard of Bingen, have left an indelible mark on spiritual literature. Their poems, writings, and teachings continue to inspire seekers to this day, inviting them to embark on their own inner journeys.

In addition to individual mysticism, certain religious traditions have mystical branches that delve into the depths of spiritual experience. In Islam, Sufism embraces the language of love and devotion, seeking a direct encounter with the Divine Beloved. Within Judaism, Kabbalah explores the hidden dimensions of the Torah and the mysteries of the divine emanations.

Mysticism also flourished in the East, with traditions like Taoism and Zen Buddhism advocating direct experience and intuitive understanding. Taoist sages sought harmony with the Tao, the fundamental principle underlying all existence, while Zen practitioners pursued enlightenment through meditation and koans, paradoxical riddles designed to provoke profound insights.

Despite the diversity of mystical paths, they share a common aspiration—to awaken to a deeper reality and to embody divine qualities such as love, compassion, and wisdom. Mysticism reminds us that our existence transcends the boundaries of time and space, and our journey of self-discovery leads us to the core of our being.

In the chapters that follow, we will explore the lives and teachings of some of history's most influential mystics. Through their stories, we will glimpse the universality of the mystical experience and its profound impact on the spiritual evolution of humanity. As we journey through the corridors of ancient wisdom, we open ourselves to the transformative power of mysticism, which continues to illuminate the path towards unity and enlightenment.

Chapter 4: Monotheistic Faiths: Finding Oneness in Diverse Beliefs

Among the world's spiritual tapestry, the monotheistic faiths stand tall as pillars of devotion to a single, all-encompassing God. While each tradition expresses unique beliefs and practices, they all share a profound commitment to the oneness of the Divine.

In Judaism, the oldest of the monotheistic religions, the belief in Yahweh as the one true God forms the bedrock of faith. The Hebrew Bible, known as the Tanakh, serves as the sacred scriptures, recounting the covenant between God and the Jewish people. The teachings emphasize justice, righteousness, and the moral responsibility of individuals to uphold ethical principles.

Christianity, emerging from the teachings of Jesus Christ, heralds the belief in the Holy Trinity—God as Father, Son (Jesus), and Holy Spirit. The life and teachings of Jesus, as recorded in the New Testament, emphasize love, compassion, and forgiveness. Christians strive to follow the example of Christ, aiming for salvation and eternal life through faith and good works.

Islam, founded by the Prophet Muhammad in the 7th century, proclaims the oneness of Allah as the central tenet. The Quran, considered the literal word of God, serves as the primary religious text. Muslims adhere to the Five Pillars of Islam, which include the declaration of faith (Shahada), prayer (Salah), charity (Zakat), fasting during Ramadan (Sawm), and the pilgrimage to Mecca (Hajj). The Islamic teachings emphasize submission to the will of God and compassion towards all beings.

Despite their shared monotheistic foundation, these faiths have witnessed both harmonious coexistence and historical conflicts. The Crusades and other religiously motivated wars bear testimony to the darker aspects of religious history. However, many followers of these traditions also advocate for peace, understanding, and interfaith dialogue, seeking to emphasize the common ground shared by all believers in one God.

Beyond the Abrahamic faiths, other monotheistic traditions also exist, such as Sikhism and Baha'i. Sikhism, founded in the 15th century by Guru Nanak, preaches belief in one God, Ik Onkar, and the importance of honest living and selfless service. The Baha'i faith, established in the 19th century by Baha'u'llah, promotes the oneness of humanity and the unity of all religions under the banner of one God.

Despite their differences, the monotheistic faiths share essential moral and ethical teachings that encourage believers to live virtuous lives. Compassion, justice, and kindness towards fellow human beings are emphasized as core values across these traditions.

In a world marked by religious diversity, the challenge for monotheistic believers lies in fostering understanding and respect for other faiths. Interfaith dialogue, driven by the recognition of shared values, allows for meaningful conversations and a deeper appreciation of diverse spiritual expressions.

While theological doctrines may differ, the shared pursuit of spiritual growth and divine connection bridges the gaps between these faiths. The universal yearning for a deeper meaning in life and the desire to align with the will of a higher power weave together the fabric of monotheism.

As we explore the depths of monotheistic beliefs, we uncover the rich history, traditions, and philosophical underpinnings that have shaped the lives of billions of people across the globe. In the chapters that follow, we will journey through the heart of these faiths, discovering the unique expressions of devotion and the profound impact they continue to have on the human experience. Through this exploration, we aim to cultivate a deeper understanding of the diverse paths leading to the one God and to embrace the unity that binds all of humanity in our spiritual quest.

Chapter 5: Eastern Philosophies: From Taoism to Zen

In the Eastern corner of the spiritual tapestry, a diverse array of philosophies and traditions await our exploration. Rooted in ancient wisdom and steeped in profound contemplation, these paths offer unique insights into the nature of existence and the human experience.

Taoism, originating in ancient China, centers around the concept of the Tao, often translated as "the Way" or "the Path." At its core, Taoism encourages harmony with the natural flow of life and the realization that the universe operates according to a cosmic order. The Tao Te Ching, attributed to the sage Laozi, serves as a foundational text, imparting the wisdom of simplicity, spontaneity, and humility.

Confucianism, also originating in China, emphasizes moral principles, social ethics, and the cultivation of virtue. The teachings of Confucius revolve around the importance of family, respect for elders, and maintaining harmonious relationships within society. Confucian thought greatly influenced the cultural and social fabric of East Asia for centuries.

Zen Buddhism, known for its contemplative practices and emphasis on direct experience, emerged in East Asia as a fusion of Indian Mahayana Buddhism and Chinese Taoism. Zen practitioners seek to attain enlightenment through meditation and intuitive understanding, often facilitated by the use of enigmatic riddles known as koans. Zen art, including calligraphy and rock gardens, embodies the simplicity and profundity of the Zen spirit.

Shinto, Japan's indigenous belief system, venerates kami, the spirits present in natural phenomena and ancestors. Shinto rituals are deeply connected to the cycles of nature, and shrines serve as sacred spaces to pay homage to the spirits. The spirit of harmony with nature and a sense of gratitude for life permeate Shinto practices.

In India, Hinduism stands as one of the world's oldest and most diverse religious traditions. The sacred scriptures, including the Vedas, Upanishads, Bhagavad Gita, and the epics Ramayana and Mahabharata, offer profound philosophical insights. Hinduism encompasses a vast array of deities, practices, and paths to spiritual realization, from the ritualistic worship in temples to the introspective practices of yoga and meditation.

Buddhism, founded by Siddhartha Gautama in India, centers around the Four Noble Truths and the Eightfold Path. These teachings address the nature of suffering, the cause of suffering, the possibility of liberation, and the path to achieving liberation (Nirvana). Buddhism spread throughout Asia, giving rise to various schools, including Theravada, Mahayana, and Vajrayana.

Jainism, also originating in India, advocates non-violence (ahimsa), non-possessiveness (aparigraha), and self-discipline as the means to spiritual liberation. Jain philosophy includes the belief in an eternal and unchanging soul (jiva) and the importance of compassion towards all living beings.

In the Eastern traditions, a strong emphasis is placed on introspection, meditation, and self-realization. The goal is to gain insight into the nature of existence, overcome suffering, and attain enlightenment or self-liberation. While some traditions emphasize devotion and ritual, others focus on direct experience and the quest for ultimate truth.

The teachings of Eastern philosophies have profoundly influenced art, literature, and culture, leaving an enduring impact on the way of life in Asia and beyond. From the poetry of the Taoist hermit to the intricacies of the Mandala in Vajrayana Buddhism, the expressions of these traditions reflect the depths of human consciousness and our interconnectedness with the cosmos.

As we explore the vast terrain of Eastern philosophies, we invite you to embrace the profound wisdom and contemplative spirit that has guided generations of seekers towards inner harmony and spiritual enlightenment. In the subsequent chapters, we will journey deeper into the heart of these traditions, unraveling the intricate tapestry of beliefs and practices that continue to shape the lives of millions across the Eastern world.

Chapter 6: Indigenous Religions: Earth-Centered Spirituality

Amidst the spiritual landscape, there exist ancient belief systems that revere the earth as sacred, cherishing the intimate connection between humanity and the natural world. These indigenous religions, nurtured by native cultures across the globe, embrace a profound sense of ecological harmony and reverence for all living beings.

Indigenous spirituality is diverse and vibrant, varying from one community to another, each deeply rooted in its unique landscape and history. From the Native American traditions of North America to the Aboriginal beliefs of Australia, and from the traditional African religions to the indigenous faiths of the Americas, these sacred paths speak to the wisdom of indigenous peoples.

At the heart of indigenous religions lies the recognition of the earth as a living entity, teeming with spirits and energy. The land, the forests, the rivers, and the mountains are all considered animate beings, deserving of respect and protection. This earth-centered spirituality manifests in rituals, ceremonies, and prayers that honor the cycles of nature and express gratitude for the gifts it provides.

Many indigenous faiths emphasize the importance of community and kinship with all living beings. The concept of "all my relations" extends beyond human connections to encompass the entire web of life. These traditions embody a holistic view of existence, where humans are regarded as equal partners with animals, plants, and the elements.

Rituals and ceremonies play a central role in indigenous spirituality, serving as bridges between the physical and spiritual realms. They mark significant events such as the changing seasons, harvests, births, and deaths, as well as acts of thanksgiving, healing, and renewal. Through dance, song, and storytelling, these rituals not only strengthen cultural identity but also foster a sense of unity with the natural world.

Ancestors hold a special place in indigenous beliefs, acting as guardians and guides for future generations. The wisdom and teachings passed down through oral traditions honor the ancestral connection and instill a sense of responsibility for preserving cultural heritage and the environment.

In the face of modern challenges such as environmental degradation and cultural erosion, indigenous communities strive to protect their sacred lands and preserve their spiritual traditions. The struggle for recognition and respect is intertwined with the fight to safeguard the earth, as these traditions teach that the well-being of the land is inseparable from the well-being of its inhabitants.

The wisdom of indigenous spirituality offers valuable insights into sustainable living and ecological harmony. Practices that align with the cycles of nature and embrace the sanctity of all life can serve as lessons for the world at large in our collective quest for environmental stewardship.

As we explore the profound wisdom of indigenous religions, we recognize the importance of preserving and respecting diverse cultural expressions. In the chapters ahead, we will delve into the spiritual richness of these communities, learning from their deep-rooted connection with the earth and their profound sense of interdependence with all living beings. Through this exploration, we hope to nurture a greater appreciation for the sacredness of the earth and embrace the wisdom that emerges from indigenous spirituality—a timeless reminder of the essential harmony between humanity and the natural world.

Chapter 7: The Quest for Enlightenment: Ascetics and Gurus

In the pursuit of spiritual growth and enlightenment, ascetics and gurus have played significant roles across various traditions. These dedicated seekers and wise teachers have inspired generations with their extraordinary commitment to inner transformation and their profound insights into the nature of existence.

Ascetics, also known as monks or renunciates, follow the path of self-denial and detachment from worldly possessions. Across different religions, ascetics withdraw from the distractions of ordinary life, choosing a life of simplicity, austerity, and meditation. By renouncing material comforts and desires, they seek to deepen their spiritual connection and attain higher states of consciousness.

In Hinduism, the ancient tradition of sannyasa calls for individuals to embrace the ascetic life after fulfilling their social and familial duties. These renunciates wander from place to place, dedicating their lives to meditation, study of scriptures, and self-realization. The sadhus of India, with their distinct appearance and unwavering commitment to spiritual practice, embody the essence of renunciation.

Buddhist monasticism is another profound example of the ascetic path. The monastic community, known as the Sangha, follows a strict code of discipline and detachment. Monks and nuns devote their lives to meditation, study of the Dharma, and the cultivation of compassion and wisdom.

In Christianity, monasticism emerged in the early centuries as a means of seeking spiritual perfection. Monks and nuns live in cloistered communities, dedicating themselves to prayer, contemplation, and a life of service to others. They strive for a deeper union with God through lives of simplicity and solitude.

Gurus, on the other hand, are spiritual guides and teachers who impart wisdom and guidance to their disciples. In various Eastern traditions, the relationship between guru and disciple is considered sacred, built on trust and devotion. The guru serves as a beacon of spiritual light, leading seekers on the path of self-discovery and realization.

In Hinduism, the guru holds a revered position as the spiritual preceptor. Through a guru's grace and guidance, a seeker can receive initiation into spiritual practices and gain profound insights into the nature of reality. The guru-disciple relationship is characterized by mutual respect, surrender, and an unwavering commitment to spiritual growth.

Sufi Islam also places great importance on the guidance of a spiritual mentor, known as a sheikh or murshid. The Sufi path is one of intense devotion and love for the Divine, and the sheikh serves as a guide, helping the disciple navigate the complexities of the heart and the soul.

In Tibetan Buddhism, the relationship between guru and disciple is vital for the transmission of esoteric teachings. The guru imparts empowerments and initiations, empowering the disciple to practice advanced meditation techniques and rituals. The Dalai Lama, as the spiritual leader of Tibetan Buddhism, embodies the essence of compassionate wisdom and serves as a guiding light for millions.

The quest for enlightenment, whether through asceticism or the guidance of a guru, is a profound and deeply personal journey. It calls for unwavering dedication, discipline, and a sincere desire to transcend the limitations of the ego and connect with the divine essence within.

In the chapters that follow, we will delve into the lives and teachings of notable ascetics and gurus from different traditions. Through their stories and wisdom, we will gain insight into the transformative power of spiritual dedication and the timeless guidance that illuminates the path to self-realization. Whether in the quietude of a monastic cell or the presence of a wise guru, the pursuit of enlightenment is a testament to the indomitable spirit of the human soul on its quest for ultimate truth and liberation.

Chapter 8: Rituals and Ceremonies: Connecting with the Divine

Rituals and ceremonies have long been intrinsic to human spirituality, serving as sacred bridges that connect the material world with the realm of the divine. Found in every culture and religious tradition, these symbolic acts provide a means of communing with higher powers, expressing gratitude, seeking protection, and marking significant life events.

The power of rituals lies in their ability to transcend the ordinary and evoke a sense of the sacred. Whether performed in grand cathedrals, humble temples, open fields, or private homes, rituals infuse the fabric of everyday life with deeper meaning and purpose.

In Christianity, the sacraments are central to the expression of faith. Baptism marks the initiation into the Christian community, signifying spiritual rebirth. The Eucharist, also known as Communion or the Lord's Supper, symbolizes the sharing of Christ's body and blood as a means of spiritual nourishment and unity with God.

In Islam, the five daily prayers (Salah) are a fundamental ritual that allows Muslims to maintain their connection with Allah throughout the day. The pilgrimage to Mecca (Hajj) is one of the most significant acts of worship, drawing millions of Muslims from around the world to partake in a profound collective spiritual experience.

Hinduism, with its rich tapestry of rituals, celebrates an array of ceremonies and festivals. From daily puja (worship) in homes to grand temple festivals and pilgrimage sites, Hindus engage in practices that honor the deities, seek divine blessings, and express devotion.

In indigenous traditions, rituals are woven into the fabric of community life. Ceremonies mark the changing seasons, honor ancestors, seek guidance from spirits, and celebrate rites of passage. From the sweat lodges of Native Americans to the dances of Aboriginal Australians, these rituals honor the interconnectedness between human beings and the natural world.

In East Asian traditions, rituals play a vital role in expressing gratitude and reverence to ancestors and deities. The ancestral worship of Confucianism, the tea ceremonies of Japan's Zen Buddhism, and the colorful celebrations of Chinese New Year are all examples of these profound acts of devotion.

Rituals often involve symbolism that conveys deeper meanings beyond words. Lighting candles, ringing bells, pouring libations, and making offerings are common elements that connect the material world with the spiritual realm. Through these rituals, believers experience a sense of continuity with their cultural heritage and a connection with the sacred traditions of their ancestors.

The transformative power of rituals extends to life's major milestones, such as birth, marriage, and death. These rites of passage mark important transitions and invoke blessings and protection for the individual or the community. From baby naming ceremonies to wedding rituals and funeral rites, these acts honor the cycles of life and the human experience.

As humanity grapples with the complexities of existence, rituals and ceremonies offer a sanctuary for reflection, solace, and celebration. They provide a sense of continuity and tradition, anchoring us in our spiritual heritage while offering opportunities for personal and communal growth.

In the chapters that follow, we will explore the diverse rituals and ceremonies from different traditions, witnessing how these sacred acts have sustained and enriched the lives of believers throughout the ages. As we immerse ourselves in the power and beauty of these rituals, we will come to understand the universality of the human quest to connect with the divine and the profound significance of these timeless acts of devotion.

Chapter 9: The Spiritual Path of Love: Devotion and Mystical Union

In the realms of spirituality, the path of love holds a special place, weaving through the hearts of devotees and mystics alike. Love, in its various expressions, serves as a transformative force, propelling seekers on a journey of devotion and mystical union with the divine.

Devotional love, known as Bhakti in Hinduism, is a powerful current that flows through many religious traditions. It is the pure and selfless love for the divine, expressed through prayers, hymns, and acts of service. Devotees see the divine in all creation and surrender their ego and desires in loving adoration.

In Hinduism, Bhakti encompasses a range of emotions, from the tender love of a child for its mother to the passionate yearning of a lover for the divine. It is embodied in the ecstatic chants of kirtan and the heartfelt prayers offered at sacred shrines. Bhakti saints like Meera, Tulsidas, and Surdas have left a profound legacy of devotion and love, inspiring generations to tread the path of the heart.

Sufism, the mystical branch of Islam, is another tradition that embraces the power of love in its quest for divine union. Sufi poets like Rumi, Hafez, and Ibn Arabi have woven eloquent verses of love, expressing their longing and surrender to the Beloved (Allah). The Sufi path is marked by a passionate love affair with the divine, seeking the annihilation of the self to attain union with the One.

Christianity also cherishes the path of love through the teachings of Jesus Christ. Love is at the heart of Christian ethics, epitomized in the commandment to "love thy neighbor as thyself." The love of Christ for humanity, symbolized by his sacrifice, serves as a profound inspiration for Christians in their journey of devotion and service.

The path of love extends beyond the Abrahamic and Dharmic traditions, finding expression in various spiritual practices worldwide. In the teachings of Buddhism, the cultivation of loving-kindness (Metta) is central to developing compassion and a sense of interconnectedness with all beings.

In the mystical traditions of Judaism, the fervent love for God is expressed in the passionate poetry of the Song of Solomon, symbolizing the intimate relationship between the soul and the Divine.

Love is not limited to human-to-divine relationships but also encompasses love for all of creation. The spiritual path of love calls for compassion towards every living being, transcending barriers of race, religion, and nationality.

Mystical union, often called "oneness" or "unity consciousness," is the culmination of the path of love. In this state of profound spiritual realization, the seeker experiences the dissolution of the self and a merging with the divine essence. Mystics throughout history have described this ecstatic union, often using the metaphor of a drop merging with the ocean.

The spiritual path of love invites seekers to open their hearts and surrender to the divine presence within and around them. It transcends dogma and doctrine, inviting believers of diverse traditions to recognize the universality of love as the essence of their spiritual journey.

In the chapters ahead, we will delve into the lives and teachings of mystics and devotees who exemplify the path of love. Their stories illuminate the transformative power of love, inspiring us to embrace the divine within ourselves and nurture a deeper connection with the world through the language of the heart. As we walk the path of love, we uncover the essence of our own being and glimpse the eternal unity that unites all creation.

Chapter 10: The Way of Wisdom: Philosophical Inquiry and Enlightenment

In the realm of spirituality, the path of wisdom beckons seekers to embark on a profound journey of philosophical inquiry and self-discovery. Rooted in the pursuit of truth and understanding, this path transcends the boundaries of religious dogma, inviting individuals to explore the nature of existence and the mysteries of the human mind.

Philosophy, from the Greek term "philosophia" meaning "love of wisdom," seeks to unravel the complexities of life, consciousness, ethics, and the cosmos. It is a quest for intellectual and spiritual enlightenment, guided by reason, logic, and critical thinking.

In ancient Greece, philosophical traditions emerged with luminaries like Socrates, Plato, and Aristotle. Socrates' method of questioning and self-inquiry laid the foundation for philosophical discourse. Plato delved into the realm of abstract ideals and the nature of reality, envisioning a world of eternal forms. Aristotle, a keen observer of the natural world, developed a systematic approach to understanding the world through empirical investigation and logical deduction.

In Eastern philosophies, the quest for wisdom is also prominent. In Confucianism, the teachings of Confucius emphasize ethical conduct, moral virtue, and the cultivation of wisdom through learning and self-reflection. Taoist philosophy, as expressed in the Tao Te Ching and Zhuangzi, explores the balance of opposites and the concept of wu wei, or effortless action.

In Buddhism, the quest for wisdom is at the heart of the Four Noble Truths and the Eightfold Path. The Buddha's teachings encourage insight into the nature of suffering, the impermanence of existence, and the path to liberation from suffering (Nirvana). The rigorous practice of meditation and mindfulness serves as a means to gain wisdom and cultivate a deep understanding of the mind and reality.

Within Hinduism, the pursuit of wisdom is embodied in the path of Jnana Yoga, the yoga of knowledge. Jnana Yoga advocates the discernment between the eternal and the transient, recognizing the self (Atman) as one with the ultimate reality (Brahman). Seekers in this path engage in self-inquiry, study of scriptures, and contemplation to attain spiritual insight.

The philosophical quest for wisdom is not limited to specific traditions but is present in various religious and spiritual paths. It is a universal call to explore the mysteries of existence and to gain deeper insights into the human condition.

In modern times, philosophy has expanded to encompass not only metaphysics and epistemology but also applied ethics, social philosophy, and political theory. The pursuit of wisdom extends beyond individual enlightenment to collective efforts to address social and ethical challenges in the world.

Wisdom is not merely an intellectual exercise but a path of moral and spiritual growth. It calls for humility, open-mindedness, and a willingness to embrace uncertainty. The philosopher, like the mystic, seeks to transcend the limitations of the ego and approach reality with a sense of wonder and awe.

In the chapters that follow, we will delve into the thoughts and wisdom of renowned philosophers, both ancient and modern, who have grappled with life's profound questions and offered insights into the nature of truth, knowledge, and the human experience. As we explore the path of wisdom, we invite you to join in the quest for a deeper understanding of the world and the profound mysteries that await the curious and reflective mind.

Chapter 11: The Dance of Creation: Exploring Sacred Art and Symbolism

In the rich tapestry of human spirituality, art has served as a powerful medium for expressing the ineffable and the sacred. Through the language of colors, forms, and symbols, sacred art transcends the limitations of words, inviting viewers to delve into the realms of mystery and spirituality.

Sacred art can be found in the majestic cathedrals of Christianity, adorned with stained glass windows and intricate sculptures that depict scenes from religious narratives. In Hindu temples, vibrant murals and sculptures celebrate the divine in its myriad forms, capturing the essence of deities and mythological stories.

Islamic art, renowned for its intricate geometric patterns and calligraphy, reflects the beauty and unity of the divine. The repetitive patterns symbolize the eternal nature of God, while the flowing calligraphy serves as a visual expression of the sacred word.

In Buddhist art, statues of the Buddha and bodhisattvas exude serene compassion, inspiring devotees on their spiritual path. Thangkas, Tibetan Buddhist paintings, are intricate works of art that convey spiritual teachings and meditative practices.

Indigenous art, deeply rooted in nature and community, often embodies the connection between humans and the natural world. From the totem poles of Native American tribes to the bark paintings of Aboriginal Australians, these artworks hold sacred significance and serve as vessels for storytelling and ancestral wisdom.

Sacred symbols, such as the cross, the lotus, the yin and yang, the om, and the mandala, transcend cultural boundaries, speaking a universal language of the divine. These symbols convey profound truths and invite contemplation, evoking a sense of unity and interconnectedness.

Beyond traditional forms, contemporary artists continue to explore sacred themes through their work. Through painting, sculpture, music, dance, and poetry, they channel the ineffable into tangible expressions, offering viewers a glimpse into the realms of the sacred.

Sacred art is not limited to the visual realm but extends to music and dance. In the mesmerizing chants of Gregorian music, the soul finds solace and elevation. In the meditative movements of whirling dervishes, the Sufis express their spiritual journey towards divine unity.

Art serves as a portal for the artist and the viewer to connect with the deeper layers of existence. It can inspire introspection, awe, and a sense of wonder. The experience of sacred art goes beyond the aesthetic appreciation, touching the heart and awakening the spirit.

The creation of sacred art is often seen as a spiritual practice itself, requiring a state of mindfulness and devotion. The artist becomes a conduit for the divine, allowing creativity to flow through them and manifest in their work.

In the chapters that follow, we will explore the diverse expressions of sacred art and symbolism, from ancient to contemporary, witnessing how these creations have enriched the spiritual experiences of humanity. As we delve into the dance of creation, we open ourselves to the profound language of sacred art, inviting its beauty and wisdom to resonate within our souls and illuminate our own spiritual journey.

Chapter 12: The Tapestry of Ethics: Living a Virtuous Life

Ethics, the study of moral principles and values, forms an essential thread in the fabric of human spirituality. Across cultures and religions, ethical teachings guide believers on the path of virtuous living, encouraging compassion, honesty, and a deep sense of responsibility towards others and the world.

In every spiritual tradition, ethical codes provide a moral compass, offering guidance on how to navigate the complexities of life with integrity and kindness. These principles call for the recognition of the inherent worth and dignity of all beings and the imperative to act in ways that promote the well-being of individuals and the community.

The Golden Rule, a universal ethical precept found in various forms across cultures, embodies the essence of ethical teachings. It encourages individuals to treat others as they would wish to be treated, fostering empathy and compassion as the foundation for ethical behavior.

In Christianity, the teachings of Jesus Christ emphasize love, forgiveness, and service to others. The Sermon on the Mount outlines a code of ethics that calls for humility, meekness, and the pursuit of righteousness. Christians are encouraged to follow the example of Christ, who demonstrated compassion towards the marginalized and forgiveness towards those who wronged him.

In Islam, the Five Pillars and the teachings of the Prophet Muhammad guide Muslims on their ethical journey. The principles of honesty, justice, and charity are central to Islamic ethics. Muslims are encouraged to show kindness and compassion towards all, and the concept of ummah, or community, underscores the interconnectedness of humanity.

Hindu ethics stem from the principles of dharma, which encompass righteousness, duty, and moral responsibility. The Bhagavad Gita, a sacred scripture, offers teachings on the ethical path, calling for selfless action and surrendering the fruits of one's actions to the divine.

Buddhism places a strong emphasis on ethical conduct as part of the Eightfold Path. The five precepts—abstaining from harming living beings, stealing, engaging in sexual misconduct, lying, and indulging in intoxicants—serve as a foundation for cultivating compassion and moral integrity.

In indigenous traditions, ethics are intertwined with a deep reverence for nature and a sense of interconnectedness with all living beings. The concept of stewardship and responsibility for the well-being of the land and its creatures underpins ethical teachings in these cultures.

Ethical teachings extend beyond the human realm to include the treatment of animals and the environment. Many spiritual traditions advocate for compassionate stewardship of the Earth and a recognition of the sacredness of all life.

In the contemporary world, the need for ethical guidance has become increasingly vital as societies grapple with complex ethical dilemmas. Issues such as environmental conservation, social justice, and technological advancements raise profound moral questions that call for ethical discernment and responsibility.

Living an ethical life requires not only adherence to principles but also inner reflection and mindfulness. It demands a willingness to examine one's actions and their impact on others, as well as the courage to make ethical choices even when they may be challenging.

In the chapters that follow, we will explore the ethical teachings of different traditions and the profound impact of living a virtuous life. Through the exploration of ethical principles, we are reminded of the interconnectedness of humanity and the responsibility we all share in shaping a more compassionate and just world. As we weave the tapestry of ethics into our lives, we contribute to the enduring legacy of moral wisdom that has guided seekers on their spiritual journeys throughout history.

Chapter 13: The Quest for Meaning: Spirituality and the Human Experience

At the heart of human spirituality lies a profound quest for meaning and purpose. As sentient beings, we grapple with existential questions that have echoed through the ages: Who am I? What is the purpose of life? What happens after death? The search for answers to these fundamental questions weaves a common thread that unites humanity in its spiritual journey.

Spirituality, in its essence, is an exploration of the deeper dimensions of existence. It calls for a recognition of the sacred within and around us, transcending the boundaries of the material world. The human experience is marked by a yearning for connection—with the divine, with others, and with the universe as a whole.

Throughout history, seekers have turned to various spiritual traditions, philosophies, and practices to find solace and meaning in the face of life's uncertainties. Whether through prayer, meditation, rituals, or contemplation, spirituality offers a sanctuary for introspection and reflection, helping individuals navigate the complexities of life and uncover the hidden truths of their existence.

In moments of joy and celebration, spirituality invites us to express gratitude for life's blessings and the interconnectedness with others. In times of sorrow and loss, it provides a source of comfort, offering hope and a sense of continuity beyond the realm of the physical.

Spirituality is not confined to any particular religion or belief system. It is a deeply personal and subjective experience that evolves as individuals journey through life. For some, spirituality finds expression through organized religion, while others explore spirituality through nature, art, or the pursuit of knowledge.

The human experience is marked by moments of awe and wonder—moments that transcend the mundane and touch the divine. Whether in the contemplation of a starry night sky, the birth of a child, or the act of creating art, these moments remind us of the mysteries and marvels of existence.

The pursuit of meaning is often intertwined with the search for inner peace and fulfillment. Spirituality invites individuals to delve into the depths of their being, cultivating self-awareness and compassion towards oneself and others. It encourages the development of virtues such as patience, kindness, and resilience.

In the modern world, as technology and material comforts abound, the quest for meaning remains as relevant as ever. Amidst the noise and distractions, spirituality offers a respite—a path towards reconnecting with the essence of our humanity and the sacredness of life.

The journey of spirituality is not linear, nor does it offer easy answers. It is a tapestry of experiences, emotions, and insights that unfold over time. The spiritual seeker is like an explorer, venturing into the uncharted territories of the soul, seeking understanding and illumination.

In the chapters that follow, we will delve into the diverse expressions of spirituality and the myriad ways in which individuals seek meaning and purpose in their lives. From the rituals of ancient traditions to the contemplative practices of modern seekers, we will witness the profound impact of spirituality on the human experience. As we embrace the quest for meaning, we embark on a journey that leads us to the depths of our being and the boundless horizons of the spiritual realm.

Chapter 14: The Unity of Humanity: Embracing Diversity and Interconnectedness

Amidst the tapestry of human spirituality, a profound truth emerges—that all of humanity is interconnected, bound by a common thread of shared existence. This realization calls for the celebration of diversity and the embrace of our universal kinship, transcending the artificial boundaries that separate us.

The beauty of human spirituality lies in its diversity, with countless colors and shades enriching the global mosaic of beliefs and practices. Across continents and cultures, diverse spiritual traditions offer unique insights into the mysteries of existence, reflecting the myriad ways in which humanity seeks to connect with the divine.

In this rich tapestry, we find the wisdom of the East, the compassion of the West, the indigenous reverence for nature, and the mystic's quest for unity. Each strand contributes to the vibrant fabric of human spirituality, reminding us that there are countless paths leading to the same truth.

The interconnectedness of humanity is evident in the shared human experience—the joys and sorrows, the triumphs and challenges that resonate in the hearts of people across the world. From birth to death, from love to loss, the human journey is marked by common threads of emotion and experience.

Yet, the diversity of human spirituality goes beyond traditions and rituals—it encompasses the kaleidoscope of individual beliefs and personal experiences. Each person's spiritual journey is unique, shaped by their culture, upbringing, and personal encounters with the sacred.

In our interconnected world, the call for understanding and respect is more crucial than ever. The richness of human spirituality is an invitation to engage in meaningful dialogue, fostering a culture of empathy and curiosity that bridges the gaps between different beliefs.

The celebration of diversity in spirituality serves as a mirror for embracing the richness of life itself. Just as a garden thrives with various flowers of different hues, the human spirit flourishes when it embraces the beauty of cultural diversity.

The interconnectedness of humanity has profound implications for our shared responsibilities as stewards of the Earth. As we recognize our unity, we must also acknowledge our collective duty to protect the planet and care for all its inhabitants.

In an age of globalization, technology, and unprecedented connectivity, we have an opportunity to draw inspiration from the universal values found in spiritual traditions across the world. Compassion, love, and justice are virtues that transcend borders and languages, uniting us as global citizens.

As we traverse the final chapters of this tapestry of spirituality, we will delve into the importance of interconnectedness and the bridges that connect humanity. Through the stories of individuals and communities, we will witness the power of unity and the transformative potential of embracing diversity.

The unity of humanity is not merely a lofty ideal; it is an invitation to weave a world of understanding, compassion, and harmony. By embracing the sacredness of all life and acknowledging our shared spiritual journey, we move closer to the realization of a world in which love and understanding prevail over division and strife. As we conclude this exploration of human spirituality, may we be inspired to cultivate the seeds of unity, empathy, and interconnectedness in our own hearts and in the tapestry of our global community.

Chapter 15: The Eternal Quest: Embracing the Journey

In the final chapter of our exploration of human spirituality, we come to recognize that the quest for meaning, connection, and enlightenment is an eternal journey—one that transcends time and space. From the ancient sages of distant civilizations to the seekers of the present day, the search for spiritual truth and understanding endures as an enduring aspect of the human experience.

The journey of spirituality is not bound by the constraints of a single lifetime. It is a continuum that extends beyond the boundaries of birth and death, inviting us to consider the timeless nature of the soul and the infinite possibilities for growth and realization.

Throughout history, spiritual seekers have walked diverse paths, each leaving footprints of wisdom and insight for future generations to follow. As we inherit the legacy of their teachings, we also become torchbearers, illuminating the way for those who come after us.

The pursuit of spirituality is not a destination, but a continuous unfolding—a dance of discovery, learning, and transformation. It is a tapestry that we weave with our thoughts, actions, and intentions, shaping our own spiritual landscape and contributing to the collective evolution of humanity.

The eternal quest calls for courage and resilience, for there are moments of doubt, uncertainty, and darkness along the way. Yet, these are the very moments that serve as catalysts for growth and self-discovery. In the depths of darkness, the light of insight often emerges, illuminating the path ahead.

The journey of spirituality invites us to embrace paradoxes and mysteries, recognizing that some questions may never have definitive answers. It calls for humility and an openness to the vastness of the unknown, acknowledging that the essence of spirituality lies in the journey itself, rather than reaching a final destination.

In the quiet moments of meditation and contemplation, we connect with the eternal realm within, touching the timeless presence that transcends the fluctuations of the material world. In these moments of communion, we glimpse the essence of our own being—the eternal soul that animates our earthly existence.

As we embrace the eternal quest, we recognize that every experience, every encounter, and every choice is an opportunity for spiritual growth. The challenges we face are not obstacles, but stepping stones that propel us towards greater awareness and understanding.

The eternal quest also reminds us of the interconnectedness of all life. We are not isolated beings, but part of a grand symphony of existence, each note contributing to the harmony of the whole.

In this concluding chapter, we reflect on the profound journey of human spirituality—a journey that spans generations, cultures, and beliefs. From the peaks of mystical experiences to the quiet moments of introspection, each step on this path deepens our connection with the sacred and enriches our understanding of ourselves and the world.

As we conclude this exploration, may we continue to embrace the eternal quest with curiosity and wonder, acknowledging that the true essence of spirituality lies not in reaching an endpoint but in the ceaseless evolution of the soul. May we walk this path with compassion and reverence, embracing the sacredness of all life and honoring the interconnectedness of humanity and the cosmos. May the eternal quest be an ever-present reminder that, in the grand tapestry of existence, we are all threads woven together in the divine fabric of creation.

Epilogue: A Tapestry of Spirituality

As we come to the end of our journey through the tapestry of human spirituality, we find ourselves standing amidst a rich mosaic of beliefs, practices, and insights. Each chapter we explored has contributed to the grand narrative of spiritual exploration that spans across cultures and civilizations. The threads of wisdom and inspiration woven together create a beautiful and intricate design, reflecting the diversity and unity of the human spirit.

In this tapestry, we have witnessed the profound impact of spirituality on the human experience. From the quest for enlightenment and the embrace of love to the exploration of sacred art and the pursuit of ethical living, spirituality has left an indelible mark on human history and continues to shape the lives of millions around the world.

We have encountered the wisdom of ancient sages and modern mystics, heard the echoes of prayers and chants, and seen the transformative power of spiritual practices and rituals. Through these diverse expressions of spirituality, we have discovered that, despite our differences, we share a common yearning for meaning, connection, and purpose.

The tapestry of spirituality is not static—it continues to evolve and adapt to the changing times. In the face of modern challenges and opportunities, spirituality remains a source of solace, guidance, and inspiration. It provides a compass in navigating the complexities of a rapidly changing world, grounding us in our shared humanity and reminding us of the sacredness of life.

As we step away from this exploration, may we carry with us the wisdom and insights gained from this journey. May we embrace the beauty of diversity and unity, recognizing that each individual's spiritual path is a unique and valid expression of their inner quest.

May we approach our own spiritual journey with curiosity and openness, inviting the mysteries of existence to unfold before us. Let us cultivate empathy and compassion, extending a hand of understanding to those who walk different paths.

As we continue to weave the tapestry of spirituality, may we be mindful of the interconnectedness of all beings and the Earth that sustains us. Let us nurture a deep reverence for life, honoring the sanctity of all living things and our shared responsibility as caretakers of this planet.

The journey of spirituality is boundless, and our exploration here is but a fragment of the infinite tapestry. As we conclude this chapter, we find ourselves standing on the threshold of new discoveries and revelations that await us in the realm of the sacred.

May the spirit of exploration and wonder guide us on this eternal quest for truth, love, and enlightenment. And as we traverse the landscapes of the human spirit, may we continue to marvel at the beauty and complexity of the tapestry of spirituality—a living testament to the boundless potential of the human soul.

Title: Harmony in Hues: Unifying Spirituality Across World Religions

A short Description of the book:
"Harmony in Hues: Unifying Spirituality Across World Religions" is a captivating and enlightening exploration of human spirituality, weaving together the diverse tapestry of beliefs, practices, and insights from various religious traditions. This profound and insightful book takes readers on a transformative journey, unveiling the common threads that unite humanity in its quest for meaning, connection, and enlightenment. From the pursuit of love and wisdom to the celebration of sacred art and the embrace of diversity, each chapter delves into the timeless and universal aspects of the human spirit. "Harmony in Hues" is a celebration of the beauty of diversity and the interconnectedness of all life, inviting readers to embark on their own spiritual journey with curiosity, compassion, and reverence. This book leaves a lasting impression, reminding us of the eternal quest for truth and the boundless potential of the human soul.

9 798854 844758